It
Start's
With
A
Desire

Proven & Tested principles to acquire Unquenchable Success in life.

Paul Edwards

To the Almighty God,
for giving us the freedom of choice
which makes available for us the
opportunity to grow a desire.

To everyone out there who desires to
make a meaning out of their lives
and impact the world at large.

TABLE OF CONTENT

Acknowledgements
Introduction

THIS PAGE IS INTENTIONALLY LEFT BLANK.

Acknowledgements

I want to use this medium to thank the wonderful family given to me by God, I want to also thank my mum for her awesome support, and I also will use this medium to appreciate my sibling for their unbending support to see the success of this work.

Introduction

Growing up we all had that one thing we wanted to become be it superheroes, or like our parents, teachers or people around us, we all one way or the other always have that longing even as we grow up, the focus may change, we might change the course of our lives, study, job, location, but all still boils down to a desire which over time has become a longing and for some an obsession, with this book in your hand we are explore how our desires, positively or negatively shape and change our lives.

THIS PAGE IS INTENTIONALLY LEFT BLANK.

Chapter One

Meaning of Desire

According to the American Heritage Desk Dictionary, the word *"DESIRE"* means to wish, too long for; want, to express a wish for, a wish or longing.

I believe the dictionary say's it all, or whatever meaning you might have given the word desire in as much it does what having desires does to a man to you, then I think you have some understanding of the word, but for the sake of better understanding, anything that makes you change decisions in a twinkle of an eye is called "DESIRE", desire can be created in a matter of seconds, by different factors which we will discuss latter on, desire is a Force built consciously or not which has in itself the ability to makes us do, react to certain things and anything in a particular manner, desires are like a pulling force in a one's life, the funny thing is that our desires we been conscious about it or not reflects in our day to day lives, through the words we speak, the choices, even in things like the food we eat, the clothes we put on, where we decide to go, how we relate with others. It our desire to be healthy and fit, that makes us hit the gym, be careful of what we eat and drink, our desire to make meaning out of lives push us to change career, the desire to please our fiancé or fiancée, make us want to look better than we are, try to always appear neat and well groomed, to talk better, and more it all the desire, the desire for either a higher pay check or a good relationship with our boss, makes us work our ass off, trying to be and do the best we can, now it's important to note that all the instances given here might not apply to you, but you can review your actions and choices and ask why am I, or why do I actually do this, it might not necessarily be a positive reason but it's always to the gratification of a desire, as simple as picking this book or any other book is as a result of the desire to be more knowledgeable, so why we stick to a bad habit is really because of the temporal satisfaction that comes along with it, so now you should know that all we do or will do is connected to our desires.

Desires per se are not necessarily bad as they are just simply forces generated from some things we will be discussing in the later part of this book.

Human wants in relation to desire

Economist made us realize that the human wants are insatiable, so you know that every human want is connected to a Desire, in fact you can say our wants are also an expression of our desires.

Types of Desires

The desire for recognition

The desire for appreciation

The desire to be loved

The desire for power

The desire for money/wealth

The desire for peaceful home

The desire for sex (intimacy)

The desire for..

The list is endless this are just most of you will find and some of our desires are actually intertwined with others or some of the ones listed here, lets discuss some of them this way we can actually see how are lives are actually shaped by something as crucial as our desires which some of us don't even pay attention too.

The desire for recognition

This is one of, if not the most powerful of all human desires, the longing for importance, recognition, a desire for attention, respect from peers, spouse, family, colleagues at work, an organization, the list is endless, we all want that sense of importance and that we are valued.

The desire for appreciation

This also is a inner longing in everyone, common who doesn't want or love to be appreciated, by parent spouse, at school, at work we all get the rush when we are appreciated, especially from either someone you are trying to please, e.g. your boss that two(2) seconds word "thank you", can really do a lot to how you feel, it can literally change your mood for the rest of the day if not days, the desire for appreciation is one of the many desires of man.

The desire to be loved

The desire to be loved is also a desire that has been with everyone right from childhood, we all want to be loved by people we love too, we want to be loved for who we are, for what we represent, and we want to be loved as we love.

The desire for power

The desire for power differs from individual to individual, but generally no one want to be made inferior, to feel inferior, or treated inferior, our ways of expressing this desire is what differs as some opt out for spiritual powers, some physical strength, some political power.

The desire for money/ wealth

This desire is one of the most practical ways for expressing our desires, both the lazy and hardworking, those who obey the principles of wealth and those who go against all have one thing in come, we still desire to be rich, we desire to be wealthy, and with the kind of world we live in presently, to survive, make impact, and more you need to be financially buoyant.

The desire for a peaceful home

No one after the day's work would love to return to a home where there's strive, or you can't have rest, or to a nagging spouse, neither do any one want to spend the rest of their lives with someone in a supposed home, where there's no peace, we all want a home where we feel at home, a home where there's love, a home where we are welcomed, appreciated, and a place we can always long for.

What influences our Desires

For man there are literally a lot of things, ranging from where we grew up, the people we grew up with, those we listened to, those we saw as mentors or role models, our peers, and as we grew, the pressure from the society and life, your boss, your environment, pain, anger, past experience, what we watch and listen to, literally everything has a say one way or the other in our lives.

Major life influences

A lot influences our lives, just as we have mentioned some earlier on in our book, but we will be discussing some of the major influencers that tend to make the most impacts in mankind

Our environments:

Our environment more than any other factor define and contribute to our desires, where we grew up, our neighborhood, the schools we attended the places we go, our home all influence our perspective about life and our desires is largely dependent on our perspective, if your grew in an rich environment where the rich is also appreciated, a happy and loving home, a good school, a lot of exemplary successful people around you to look up to, and everyone in one way or the other is working on making a better life for themselves, their families, there love and unity in that environment, you will grow up not just with the desire to be rich too, but you will also want to be appreciated, you will grow to see the value for hard work and discipline and you would love to live where there's love and peace also, and reverse is the case for someone who grew in an environment where the rich and successful are seen as thieves or an extremely poor environment, or an environment, where there's strive and unrest, crime is the order of the day, you might not necessarily grow up to be a criminal yourself, but the fact that you grew up in such a neighborhood, in my country there's a saying "you can take the boy out of the village, but you can't take the village out of him.", how true is this, not just a village, it's the same everywhere, our environments do a lot to what we desire and how we see life in general.

Those we listen to:

We all have people around us, but been specific now to those we listen to, listen to in term of those you take advice from, those you see as an example and you can consult on certain subject matter, they also play a major role in our lives and in our desires too, for someone you take advice from on the subject of finance for example, family life/parenting, his or her one life has become a yardstick for you to live up, you are not limited to their level, but you have to get to their level first, and the fact that you take advices from them and all, they teach or advice you based on their perspective of life or on the subject you seek advice for, they impact in you their principles, it more or less you start reliving their lives, so you can become like them, you definitely won't want to take advice from who you don't want to be like, so now we you see how those we listen to shape how desires and at large our lives.

The books we read:

Books most times are the minds of people, documented lives of people, and the thoughts of people on different subjects, when we read books we read into the minds of the author, and we digest their thoughts and believes, their thinking and this play a huge role also in the way we begin to see things, and also it influences our desires too. Great books build your mind greatly, gives you a paradigm shift and you begin to desire great if not greater outcome out of your life, that is why readers are called leaders. Books expose you to various thinking on a particular matter, from different minds, and from people who are undergoing and have different experiences.

Past experiences (pain, anger):

Experience some times is said to be the best teacher, what we pass through has a way of molding us, and our desires too are not left out of the molding, common drives like pain and anger are major drives through which our experiences are reflected and a new desire can be the result, and these can be positive and negative at times, but the point we are driving at is the birthing of new desires or shaping of our past desires.

Chapter Two

Vision in co-relation to Desire

The word vision has been given a lot of meaning, and not limited by the context of usage, the definition or interpretation of the word are still similar "VISION" simply put can be called seeing into a possibility, a foresight of what can be from what is not presently, our desires on the long term basis though can also be referred to as a vision, a student who desires to be a medical doctor in the nearest future is already envisioning himself/herself practicing, in a big hospital attending to patients already, a child who desires to be wealthy or a teen who loves basketball and desires to go pro is already imagining (seeing) himself as the next Kobe Bryant, Michael Jordan, etc. A vision is where you are not but "desire" to be.

Our imagination/ the mind

The mind is the most powerful tool available to man, you can make and mar yourself with your mind, the way our mind works is why it house the vision, the mind sees, that why we have the concept of imagination, which is basically seeing what is not or not yet a reality, our vision is more or less an imagination, a desire that is imagined, no matter what is desired it comes as an imagined possibility.

The mind is a great tool at our disposal, you should strive to make the maximum use of it, and this is not to motivate you or any such thing, whatever you can dream (see) with your mind, you can become, whatever you can imagine, whatever you can desire you can have, if you see it, truly you can be it. Your reality is first created with your mind before it can become visible.

A popular saying goes thus "you are what you think about most of the time."

The price to make our desire come true

The price is simple, it's just not easy to implement and be consistent with, and the price is "Discipline" you might ask discipline you say, yes that the simple truth we all know or at least have heard of, yet only a very small percentage of mankind really put this to work in their lives to achieve their desired results, discipline is basically you doing what you should do, when you should do it whether you want to do it or not, discipline is you letting the future you (who you aspire to become) have a say in all you do, how do I mean you may ask, let's drive right in, when confronted with the choice to the careless with money, skip the gym or consume more of sugar and junk, the future you whom you desire to be a very wealthy and healthy person will never compromise on his/her standards, on living right, eating right, and more, that the way you should start living your life now, be disciplined with your time, resources, your dreams are not cheap, so don't expect the price to be cheap, work so hard every day like there's no tomorrow to work again, and let this new habit or lifestyle of your compound over time and you will marvel at how far you have gone ahead.

Choose your pain.

Choose your pain, this phrase carries the inspiration you need to live, as the you, you love to become, helping you live a better life. (Finding your pain is you finding your reason for doing, for taking action for the unbending focus.). choosing your pain Is the like a driving force that keeps you going that for instance because of the agony you saw your father go through because of smoking after his kidney and liver has finally been destroyed, that pain of watching him becomes your motivation never to smoke in your life no matter what, or another instance the increasing debts and reproach that comes with poverty, will leading you to do all it takes to work extremely hard to achieve financial freedom.

Your pain in this context refers to your "why", have you asked yourself why I want to be successful, why do I want this why I want that, pain comes in when there are actually life personal experiences. Your reason for wanting to be a great father who would a legacy for a children, your pain could be you having a father who was never there for you, your reason for wanting to be an exceptionally rich, might be as the result of the pain of growing up in poverty. Pain is a great driver, a great motivation at times, uses your pain to your advantage.

There are a lot of pains that can serve as motivation to you, that can serve as a driving force to be disciplined and focused. Yeah it's pain its not something great right but since you couldn't avoid it maximize it, for your future, your family, your children and the world at large.

Other factors that can be a pain in the ass and becomes a driving force parental limitation, insult from the society, growing up in a debt owing family, environment, people attitudes.

Chapter Three

Channeling our desires for our growth

Our desires are ours and should be for our own good, it should be for our own wealth, happiness, not the other way round. But this doesn't just happen as we have learnt earlier things that tend to help shape our desires through the people, environment, books we interact with, which can be positive or negative.

In this chapter we will learn how to consciously channel how desires and make the better use of it.

Conscious decision making.

This is needed if you truly want to make your desires yours (for who you want to be and not for what your flesh wants presently), conscious decision making is required if we truly want to influence our desires and not the other way round.

What is decision making:
Decision making is basically making a choice, going for an option out of many options or choices.

Conscious decision making:
Conscious decision making is making a choice or taking an option with the end result, consequences in view and been ready to live with the outcome of that decision.

The steps which will help us channel our desires for our growth requires conscious decision making from our path.

Steps to channeling our desires for our growth:
Knowing who you want to be:
Having a clear direction of who you desire, how you want to end up 30, 40 50, 60 years from now is a great step to channeling your desires for growth, imagining a life with all your wishes

fulfilled the joy that comes with it and also imagining your life the opposite of what you wanted it to be and the pain, regrets that comes with it. With this in mind, your desires comes first before your actions so consciously channel your desires towards who you want to be and create a longing for it, then you find yourself taking actions towards who you want to be.

Choose your friends/those you associate with, don't let them choose you:

A popular saying also says "show me your friends and I can tell you who you are". The people you associate with day in day out have a way of influencing your life, influencing your perspective about life, influencing your behavior and basically your desires are also influenced alongside, and when your associates, friends are not going in the direction that will aid you become the better version of yourself, then that is a wrong association, that is why you should choose your friends, and not the other way round, that way before you choose you have taken your time to see that your relationship with this person will definitely influence you but the influence is to your advantage that is the influence he/she will have on you will help you become a better you.

Carefully select your mentors:

mentors are those you have given a right to serve as a watch, guardian, advisor over your life, there's no reason you shouldn't be careful when selecting one and you don't select mentors because they are good or nice people, or basically just adults, mature, you select mentors based on your vision, based on who you want to become, knowing full well that whoever should serve as a mentor in your life will be able to advise you, direct you on the path you have chosen, most times selecting a mentor who has walked the path you choose to tread is best, carefully choose your mentors, their advices and instructions to you become a desire, an action which you commit to do and if those advice does not get you closer to who you want to be then that person whoever he/she is, is not worth to be your mentor.

Carefully select the books you read, what you feed your eyes and ears to:

The ears and eyes are windows into the soul and what they are fed consistently that tell the end of a man, or rather how a man will end, the content will feed ourselves influences our desires, now to channel that for our advantage is by consciously selecting the books we read the, TV channel we watch, the podcasts, tapes we listen to, we need to be committed to growth give no room for mediocrity or slacking, day in day out let it become an obsession to be a better version of myself daily, with this in mind carefully select the podcast that helps you grow, carefully select the books that on a daily brings you closer to who you want to be, Tv on its own is an addiction that if possible should be totally cut out but while not cut out the content you feed your mind should be growth focused, growth oriented, same with social media, do just waste time doing nothing but scrolling through pages on social media, the internet has its advantages and you should use it to your advantage.

Find out the areas you want to address in your life and get content that proffer solution in that area, if it be finances, health, marriage, career, go for knowledge they are readily available change your life for yourself, not for anyone.

Discipline:

Discipline they say is the mother of all good qualities, none of the principles mentioned above will work if the subject does not make up his/her mind to be committed to growth, committed to change, nothing will really change if you don't decide to discipline yourself alongside, look at it you want to change your life, you want to get better, you want to recreate yourself, your life, recall you had a lifestyle, a life pattern before, a way of life before which you want to change, that old self will not go without a fight, without resistance that old lifestyle was built over years of repeating the same habits, associating with the same people and reacting, behaving in a particular pattern, so you should know you won't just change overnight, you probably will relapse more than once but prepare for war too, its war against the me I don't want, so you have to fight it and fight it hard, and you surely will win, you will change, you will desire the best things for you,

you will act according to you want with a goal in mind daily becoming the better you.

ABOUT THE AUTHOR

Paul Edwards is a personal and career growth strategist, a wealth creation catalyst, human development coach, author, transformational speaker, whose interest right from a young age, has been on personal success and achievements, he is an astute investor with diverse investment across various industries.

His main focus has been to live an inspirational life that reveals to other that you can be all you desire to be no matter where you are presently all you need is to decide to, and also to help raise others, help them achieve the life they want and also help them show others how.

www.ingramcontent.com/pod-product-compliance
Lightning Source LLC
Chambersburg PA
CBHW072057230526

45479CB00010B/1112

* 9 7 9 8 3 3 4 8 7 4 0 0 8 *